THE GREAT SONGS OF
COLE PORTER

CONTENTS

OLD FASHIONED GARDEN

Words and Music by
COLE PORTER

LET'S MISBEHAVE

Words and Music by
COLE PORTER

If you want a fu-ture, darl-ing, why don't you get__ a past?

'Cause that fa-tal mo-ment's com-in', at last.

REFRAIN

We're all a-lone__ No chap-er-one__ Can get our num-ber,
It's get-ting late__ And while I wait,__ My poor heart aches on,

The world's in slum-ber, Let's mis-be-have!__
Why keep the brakes on? Let's mis-be-have!__

I CONCENTRATE ON YOU

Words and Music by
COLE PORTER

When-ev-er the win-ter-winds be-come too strong,

I con-cen-trate on you.

When for-tune cries "nay, nay!" to me

And peo-ple de-clare "You're through,"

LET'S DO IT
(Let's Fall In Love)

Words and Music by
COLE PORTER

Refrain
p-mf gracefully

1 Birds do it,— Bees do it,— E-ven ed-u-cat-ed fleas do it,— Let's do it,— Let's fall in— love.—
2 Spon-ges, they— say, do it,— Oy-sters, down in Oy-ster Bay, do it,— Let's do it,— Let's fall in love.—

In Spain, the best up-per— sets do it,—
Cold Cape Cod clams, 'gainst their— wish, do it,—

Lith - u - an - i - ans and Letts do it,— Let's do it,—
Ev - en laz - y Jel - ly-fish do it,— Let's do it,—

Let's fall in— love.———————— The Dutch in old Am - ster -
Let's fall in— love.———————— E - lect - ric eels, I might—

dam do it,— Not to men - tion the Finns Folks in Si -
add, do it,— Though it shocks 'em I know. Why ask if—

LOVE FOR SALE

Words and Music by
COLE PORTER

When the on-ly sound in the

emp-ty street Is the hea-vy tread of the hea-vy feet That be-

long to a lone-some cop, I _____ o - pen

I've been thru the mill of love; Old love, new love,

Ev-'ry love but true love. Love _____ for

sale, _____ Ap-pe-tiz-ing young love for

sale. _____ If you want to buy my wares,

C'EST MAGNIFIQUE

Words and Music by
COLE PORTER

*Pronounced "say man-yee-fee-kuh"

I'M GETTING MYSELF READY FOR YOU

Words and Music by
COLE PORTER

After You

Words and Music by
COLE PORTER

MY LONG AGO GIRL

Words and Music by
COLE PORTER

Refrain.

Long, long a - go, long, long a - go under a syc - a-more tree, A maid - en said she could grow fond of me, But one sum - mer day,

RIDIN' HIGH

Words and Music by
COLE PORTER

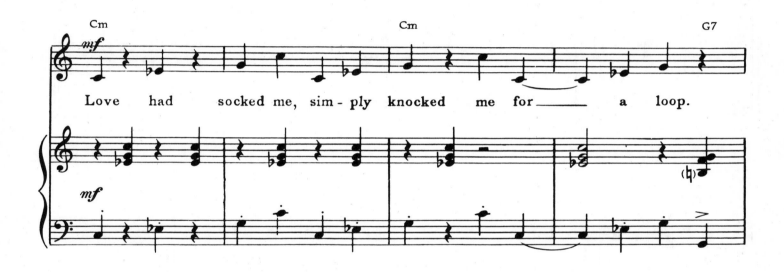

Love had socked me, sim-ply knocked me for ____ a loop.

Luck has dished me Till you fished me from ____ the soup.

YOU DO SOMETHING TO ME

Words and Music by
COLE PORTER

Some-thing that sim-ply mys-ti-fies me.

Tell me, why should it be

You have the pow'r to hyp-no-tize me?

Let me live 'neath your spell,

TWO LITTLE BABES IN THE WOOD

Words and Music by
COLE PORTER

There's a tale of two lit-tle or-phans who were left in their un-cle's care, To be

54

TRUE LOVE

Words and Music by
COLE PORTER

58

IT'S ALL RIGHT WITH ME

Words and Music by
COLE PORTER

BLOW, GABRIEL, BLOW

Words and Music by
COLE PORTER

66

REFRAIN

68

IT'S BAD FOR ME

Words and Music by
COLE PORTER

Moderato

Your words go through and through me, And leave me to-tal-ly dazed. For they

do such strange things to me, They near-ly make me gloom-y, For

you, dear, are so clev-er, So ob-vious-ly the "top," I

MISS OTIS REGRETS
(She's Unable To Lunch Today)

Words and Music by
COLE PORTER

DO I LOVE YOU
(From "Dubarry Was A Lady")

Words and Music by
COLE PORTER

ALL THROUGH THE NIGHT

Words and Music by
COLE PORTER

EXPERIMENT

Words and Music by
COLE PORTER

FROM THIS MOMENT ON

Words and Music by
COLE PORTER

THE GREAT INDOORS

Words and Music by
COLE PORTER

99

DREAM DANCING

Words and Music by
COLE PORTER

When shades en-fold The sun - set's gold And stars are bright a - bove a - gain, I smile, sweet-heart, For then I know I can start to live a-gain, to love a-gain.

MISTER AND MISSUS FITCH

Words and Music by
COLE PORTER

NIGHT AND DAY

French version by
EMÉLIA RENAUD

Words and Music by
COLE PORTER

Thank You So Much
MISSUS LOWSBOROUGH-GOODBY

Words and Music by
COLE PORTER

Allegretto

Mis-sus

Lows-bor-ough-Good-by gives week-ends ___ And her week-ends are not a suc-

cess, ___ But she asks you so of-ten, You fi-nal-ly soft-en and

Lyrics:

end by an-swer-ing "Yes." When I left Mis-sus Lows-bor-ough-

Good-by's,___ The let-ter I wrote was po-lite;___ But it

would have been bliss, Had I dared write her this, The let-ter I want-ed to write:

Thank you so much Mis-sus Lows-bor-ough-Good-by, Thank you so much,

114

Thank you so much for that in-fi-nite week-end with you. _____ Thank you a lot, Mis-sus Lows-bor-ough-Good-by, thank you a lot; And don't be sur-prised if you sud-den-ly should be qui-et-ly shot For the

taught me back-gam-mon, For those morn-ings I spent with your dear but deaf moth-er, For those

eve-nings I passed with that bound-er, your broth-er, And for mak-ing me swear to my-

self there and then Nev-er to go for a week-end a-gain.

Thank you so much Mis-sus Lows-bor-ough-Good-by, thank you, thank you so much!_

You're the Top

Words and Music by
COLE PORTER

REFRAIN

You're the top!
You're the top!
You're Ma-
Co - los - se - um,
hat - ma Ghan-di,
You're the top!
You're the top!
You're the Louvr' Mu - se - um,
You're Na - po - leon brand-y,
You're a
You're the
mel - o - dy___ From a sym-pho-ny___ by Strauss, You're a
pur - ple light_ Of a sum - mer night__ in Spain, You're the

Mo - na Lis - a; I'm a worth - less check, a
Der - by win - ner, I'm a toy bal - loon that is

to - tal wreck, a flop, But if
fat - ed soon to pop;

Ba - by, I'm the bot - tom, You're the top!

top!

MY HEART BELONGS TO DADDY
(From "LEAVE IT TO ME")

Words and Music by
COLE PORTER

124

THE PHYSICIAN
(But He Never Said He Loved Me)

Words and Music by
COLE PORTER

WHY SHOULDN'T I?

Words and Music by
COLE PORTER

stud-ied love dis-creet-ly, But now that I'm com-plete-ly free, I must

find some kind per-son-a gra-ta To give me

da-ta per-son-al-ly.

REFRAIN *Slowly, with tender expression*

Why should-n't I take a chance when ro-mance pass-es by,

ANOTHER OP'NIN', ANOTHER SHOW

Words and Music by
COLE PORTER

136

I HAPPEN TO LIKE NEW YORK

Words and Music by
COLE PORTER

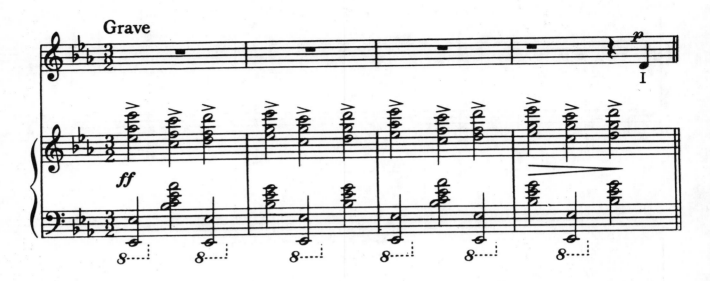

139

THE LAZIEST GAL IN TOWN

Words and Music by
COLE PORTER

REFRAIN *Slow and languid*

la-zi-est gal__ in town. My poor heart is ach-in'__ To

bring home the ba-con,__ And if I'm a-lone and for-sa-ken,__ It's

sim-ply be-cause I'm the la-zi-est gal__ in town.

Though I'm more than will-ing to learn__ How these gals get

I LOVE PARIS

Words and Music by
COLE PORTER

Ev-'ry time I look down on this time - less town, wheth-er blue or grey be her skies, Wheth-er loud be her cheers, or wheth-er soft be her tears, more and

148

Par - is in the win - ter, when it driz - zles,

I love Par - is in the sum - mer, when it siz - zles,

Sostenuto *(jubilantly)*

I love Par - is ev - 'ry mo - ment, _____

ev - 'ry mo - ment of the

I'VE GOT YOU UNDER MY SKIN

Words and Music by
COLE PORTER

Allegretto Sostenuto

I've got you __ un-der my skin, __ I've

got you __ deep in the heart of me, __ So

deep in my heart, __ You're real-ly a part of me. __ I've

I GET A KICK OUT OF YOU

Words and Music by
COLE PORTER

A PICTURE OF ME WITHOUT YOU

Words and Music by
COLE PORTER

159

REFRAIN
slowly

Pic - ture Hen - ri Ford _____ with - out a car,
Pic - ture H. G. Wells _____ with - out a brain,

p *a tempo (grazioso)*

Pic - ture Heav - en's fir - ma - ment _____ with - out a star,
Pic - ture Av' - rill Har - ri - man _____ with - out a train,

Pic - ture Fritz - y Kreis - ler with - out a fid - dle,
Pic - ture Tin - tern Ab - bey with - out a clois - ter,

Pic - ture poor Phi - la - del - phi - a with - out a Bid - dle, ___
Pic - ture Bil - ly the Oys - ter - man with - out an oys - ter, ___

WHAT IS THIS THING CALLED LOVE?

Words and Music by
COLE PORTER

WUNDERBAR
(From "KISS ME KATE")

Words and Music by
COLE PORTER

168

169

EASY TO LOVE

Words and Music by
COLE PORTER

Andantino

I know too well that I'm ____ just wast-ing pre - cious time in

think-ing such a thing could be, That you ____ could ev - er care for me,

I'M IN LOVE

Words and Music by
COLE PORTER

Refrain

GET OUT OF TOWN

Words and Music by
COLE PORTER

The farce was end - ed, The cur - tains drawn,

And I at least pre - tend - ed That love was dead and gone.

180

FIND ME A PRIMITIVE MAN

Words and Music by
COLE PORTER

183

REFRAIN

FIND ME ____ A PRIM-I-TIVE MAN ____ Built on ____

a prim-i-tive plan; ____ Some one ____ with

vig-or and vim, ____ I don't mean the kind that be-longs to a club, But the

kind that has a club that be-longs to him, I could be ____ the per-son-al slave ____

I LOVE YOU

Words and Music by
COLE PORTER

If a love song I could on-ly write,____ A song with words and

mu-sic di - vine____ I would ser - e - nade you ev - 'ry

night ____ Till you'd re-lent and con-sent to be mine ____ But a-

188

PAREE
What Did You Do To Me?

Words and Music by
COLE PORTER

194

YOU'D BE SO NICE TO COME HOME TO
(From "SOMETHING TO SHOUT ABOUT")

Words and Music by
COLE PORTER

Allegretto comodo

It's not that you're fair- er, Than a lot of girls just as pleas-in', That I doff my hat as a wor-ship-per at your shrine,— It's

BEGIN THE BEGUINE

Spanish Version by
MARIA GREVER

Words and Music by
COLE PORTER

When they be-gin ___ the Be - guine ___ It brings back the sound ___
Rit-mo an-he-lan - - - te de a - mor ___ Que sir - ve de sen -

___ of mu-sic so ten - der, ___ It brings back a night ___ of trop-i-cal
- da a la me-lo - di - a ___ Que me ha he-chool-vi-dar ___ mi me-lan-co-

splen - dour, ___ It brings back a mem - o-ry ev - er green.
-li - a ___ Tra - yen-do a mi men - te un nue-vo i - de-al

203

IN THE STILL OF THE NIGHT

Words and Music by
COLE PORTER

Take Me Back to Manhattan

Words and Music by
COLE PORTER

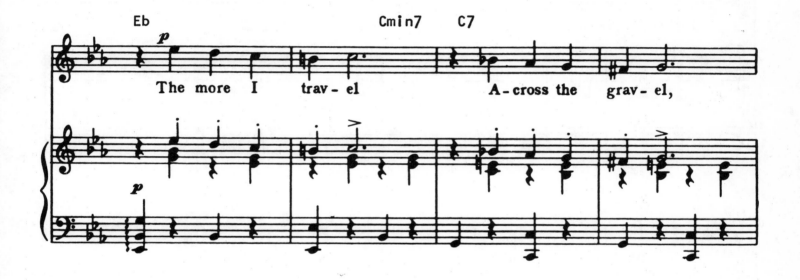

The more I trav-el A-cross the grav-el,

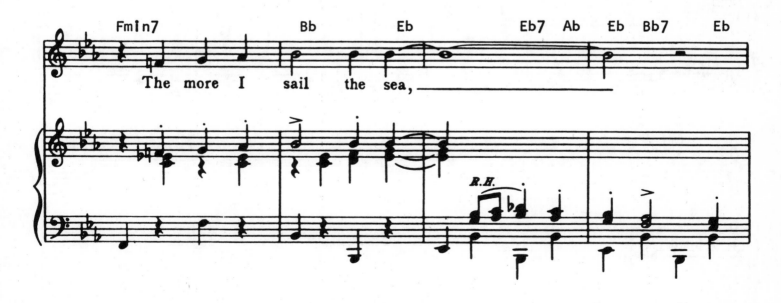

The more I sail the sea, _____

214

SO IN LOVE
(From "KISS ME KATE")

Words and Music by
COLE PORTER

JUST ONE OF THOSE THINGS

Words and Music by
COLE PORTER

223

EV'RYTHING I LOVE

Words and Music by
COLE PORTER

I hap - pen to know it, But an - y - way,_ Here's a

roun - de - lay,_ That I wrote last night a - bout you.

Refrain (*slowly, with expression*)

You are to me ev - 'ry -

thing, My life to be, ev - 'ry -

THE QUEEN OF TERRE HAUTE

Words and Music by
COLE PORTER

Tempo di Valse moderato

My moth-er and fath-er Once went to a lot of both-er To make me the hap-pi-est of girls. To bet-ter my sta-tion They gave me an ed-u-ca-tion, Not to men-tion a

Refrain

Why could-n't I have been Sa - lo - me,___ Or Ma-ry Pick - ford,___ Or Joan of Arc? ___ If I were El - 'nor Glynn, Or e-ven Anne Bo - leyn, The fu - ture would-n't look half so dark.___

* *Open strings*

Why could-n't I be Whist-ler's moth - er?___ Or an - y

oth - er wo-man of note?_____ Why did the gods de -

cree That I should on - ly be The Queen of Ter - re

Haute?_____ Haute?_____

YOU'RE SENSATIONAL

Words and Music by
COLE PORTER

He: A thor-ough know-ledge I've got a-bout girls, I've been a round
She: A thor-ough know-ledge I've got a-bout boys, I've been a round

And af-ter learn-ing a lot a-bout_ girls,
And af-ter learn-ing a lot a-bout_ boys,

This is the im-port-ant fact I found:
This is the im-port-ant fact I found:

ALL OF YOU

Words and Music by
COLE PORTER

238

YOU'VE GOT THAT THING

Words and Music by
COLE PORTER

242

ANYTHING GOES

Words and Music by
COLE PORTER

REFRAIN

DON'T FENCE ME IN

Words and Music by
COLE PORTER

AT LONG LAST LOVE

Words and Music by
COLE PORTER

love,___ I've no sense of val - ues_ left at all.___ Is this a

play - time_ af-faire of May - time, Or is it a wind - fall?___

Refrain *slowly, with warm expression*
Is it an earth quake___ or sim - ply a shock?___

___ Is it the good tur - tle soup or mere - ly the

YOU DON'T KNOW PAREE

Words and Music by
COLE PORTER

Refrain Rubato